STEPS TO FREEDOM

DOUGLAS WEISS, PH.D.

STEPS TO FREEDOM © 1997
by Douglas Weiss, Ph.D.

Requests for information:

Discovery Press
heart2heart@xc.org
719-278-3708

All rights reserved.
No part of this publication may be reproduced, stored in a retrieval system, or transmitted in any form or by any means electronic, mechanical, photocopy, recording, or any other except for brief quotations in printed reviews, without the prior permission of the publisher.

Cover and Interior Design by Janelle Evangelides
Edited by Pauli Rancourt

CONTENTS

STEP		PAGE
1	"We admitted we were powerless over our sexual addiction--that our lives had become unmanageable."	7
2	"Came to believe that a Power greater than ourselves could restore us to sanity."	19
3	"Made a decision to turn our will and our lives over to the care of God as we understood Him."	29
4	"Made a searching and fearless moral inventory of ourselves."	39
5	"Admitted to God, to ourselves, and to another human being the exact nature of our wrongs."	49
6	"Were entirely ready to have God remove all these defects of character."	61
7	"Humbly asked Him to remove our shortcomings."	71
8	"Made a list of all people we had harmed, and became willing to make amends to them all."	79
9	"Made direct amends to such people wherever possible, except when to do so would injure them or others."	85
10	"Continued to take personal inventory and when we were wrong promptly admitted it."	95
11	"Sought through prayer and meditation to improve our conscious contact with God as we understood Him, praying only for the knowledge of His will for us and the power to carry that out."	101
12	"Having had a spiritual awakening as the result of these Steps, we tried to carry this message to others, and to practice these principles in all our affairs."	107

INTRODUCTION

The Twelve Steps have helped millions of people recover from alcohol, drugs, food, sex, and many other addictions. This workbook takes individuals thoughtfully through a personal recovery from sexual addiction. These steps allow you to work at your own pace or with others from your Twelve Step support group. Our prayer and wish for you is that you will experience hope and strength throughout your personal journey to recovery so you can experience the joy that Christ has promised you.

Other materials available through Heart to Heart Counseling Center which may be helpful in your recovery are listed in the Appendix of this book. Telephone counseling through Heart to Heart Counseling Center is also available nationwide.

Please contact us for further information. You can also visit us on our website at www.sexaddict.com for access to free weekly newsletters for addicts and their partners.

Heart to Heart Counseling Center
719-278-3708
heart2heart@xc.org

"We admitted we were powerless over our sexual addiction and that our lives had become unmanageable."

⇒ WE

When asked how to pray, Jesus said "Our Father." Jesus understood the need for us to have a corporate vision rather than an individual perspective of God. When the apostle Paul wrote the "One Anothers" (Gal. 5:13, Col. 3:12-13), he understood the need that believers have for each another. Jesus' brother James also understood this when he penned James 5:16, "Confess your faults one to another, and pray one for another, that ye may be healed."

There is healing and spiritual power available as you follow the "we" principle in your life. This is especially true as you take the journey through recovery from sex addiction. Sex addicts generally enjoy doing things by themselves. In recovery, "we" is a new concept for the sex addict. As a group, "we" can do a lot more than that which can be done alone. Together "we" can heal. When we are left alone, it seems we often stay locked into our sexual addiction. We have tried recovery by ourselves with little success, but we can heal together.

We is one of the most important words that this 12 step recovery program has to offer. It is in admitting to ourselves that we are powerless over our sexual addiction and need this new "we group" that we can stay sober or clean. The sex addict has often had other "we groups" before recovery. This is our first topic of discussion.

What are some of the first words that come to your mind when you hear the word we?

1._____ 2._____ 3._____

What would you hope to gain from a clean we group?

1._____ 3._____

2._____ 4._____

What kind of peer we groups do you have in your life presently?

1._____ 3._____

2._____ 4._____

In the past, have your we groups (your friends) been other sex addicts or sex partners? List them and tell why they were in your we groups?

Sex Addicts/Sex Partners	Why?
1._____	1._____
2._____	2._____
3._____	3._____

The concept of we can be especially hard for sex addicts because many have lived much of their lives isolating themselves and their behaviors from others. When you come into a twelve step group you will experience that "we" is truly obtainable. There are other people who struggle with the same issues as you.

What are some of the feelings you have realizing that you are not alone in this recovery program?

I felt _____ when _____

When you realize you are not alone in your sexual addiction recovery, a feeling of being known and still being accepted can energize you to the point where you desire to stay in your twelve step group.

What are some of the strengths you can see this new we group adding to your sexual addiction recovery?

1._____ 3._____

2._____ 4._____

What are some of the struggles you anticipate about opening up to a group, being honest about your sexually addictive behavior, and letting them support you?

1._____

2._____

3._____

Shame over past behavior or not feeling loved (i.e., "If they really knew me, they wouldn't love me" or "I'm not worth helping. You don't know what I did.") can really slow down recovery. The next exercise will assist you in preventing those thoughts from taking over and undermining the progress in your recovery program.

What goals can you set to deal with shame so it doesn't prevent you from being a part of this important recovery we group?

1._____

2._____

3._____

4._____

What other types of we groups do you need in your life to stay clean? (Circle)

Alcoholics Anonymous	Incest Survivors	Narcotics Anonymous
Narcotics Anonymous	CODA	Over-Eaters Anonymous
Other _____	Other _____	Other _____

⇒ ADMITTED

Admitted means to acknowledged what already is a fact. We need to admit before we can become and stay clean. In Step One, what are you trying to admit to yourself that is probably already a known fact to others?

1._____

2._____

3._____

Who else may already know any or all of these facts?

1._____

2._____

3._____

4._____

How do they already know what you are admitting about yourself? (For each person listed, give examples of how they may already know about your sexual addiction.)

1._____

2._____

3._____

4._____

5._____

Admitting your sexual addiction is one of the hardest things you will ever do! What are some of the feelings you are having about admitting you are a sex addict?

I feel _____

I feel _____

I feel _____

Until now, what has kept you from admitting to yourself that you are a sex addict?

1. _____
2. _____
3. _____

Over what particular sexual behaviors are you admitting that you are currently powerless?

1. _____
2. _____
3. _____
4. _____
5. _____

How long have you been addicted to these behaviors? (Example: Self sex, 15 years)

1. _____
2. _____
3. _____
4. _____

➡ POWERLESS

Powerlessness is a state of being that many people do not really accept or even acknowledge. Sometimes we do not even admit that we are powerless in the presence of overwhelming facts.

What are some facts that lead you to believe that you are powerless over your sexual addiction?

1. _____
2. _____
3. _____
4. _____

What does it mean to you to be powerless over your sexual addiction? Define powerless.

_____

_____

What do you think being powerless over your addiction will mean to you in the future?

1._____

2._____

3._____

List the people you know are powerless over their sexual addiction?

1._____ 3._____

2._____ 4._____

Name people who will try to convince you that you are not a sexual addict.

1._____ 3._____

2._____ 4._____

How do you intend to respond to those who will try to convince you that you are not a sex addict?

1._____

2._____

3._____

4._____

What four behaviors demonstrate that you are presently powerless over your addiction?

1._____ 3._____

2._____ 4._____

If you are unable to list four behavior patterns that presently reflect your powerlessness, why do you believe you are powerless over your sexual addiction?

_____

_____

_____

What benefits do you see in being powerless over your sexual addiction?

1. _____
2. _____
3. _____
4. _____
5. _____

How do you feel about being powerless over your sexual addiction? Why?

I feel _____ because _____

How is being powerless over your sexual addiction going to affect the boundaries you set for yourself?

1. _____
2. _____
3. _____
4. _____
5. _____

How is being powerless over your addiction going to affect friendships or other relationships?

1. _____
2. _____
3. _____
4. _____

How is being powerless over your sexual addiction going to affect your sexual relationship?

1. _____
2. _____
3. _____
4. _____

What are other words that describe powerless to you?

1. _____ 3. _____
2. _____ 4. _____

Realizing that you are powerless over your addiction is a big step toward recovery. In taking this step, you will be forced to consider changes in your life, your activities, and even the boundaries you set. How is being powerless over your sexual addiction going to affect your life?

1. _____
2. _____
3. _____
4. _____
5. _____

How is being powerless over your sexual addiction going to change the activities in your life?

1. _____
2. _____
3. _____
4. _____
5. _____

How is being powerless going to affect your entertainment? (T.V., movies, books, parties, other activities)

1. _____
2. _____
3. _____
4. _____
5. _____

What other things or relationships are you powerless over other than your sexual addiction?

1. _____
2. _____
3. _____

⇒ UNMANAGEABLE

Unmanageable is another word we often do not like to hear in our culture. We take pride in being in control. List ways your addiction made you lose control in the following areas of your life.

Spiritual life

1. _____
2. _____
3. _____

Family relationships

1. _____
2. _____
3. _____

Financial areas

1. _____
2. _____
3. _____

Friendships

1. _____
2. _____
3. _____

Relationship with yourself

1. _____
2. _____
3. _____

Your future

1. _____
2. _____
3. _____

Vocationally

1. _____
2. _____
3. _____

Your spouse

1._____
2._____
3._____

Give examples of when you were unmanageable in your sexual addiction. (Be as specific as possible.)

1._____
2._____
3._____
4._____
5._____

What has your addiction cost you? (Other than money)

1._____
2._____
3._____
4._____

What feelings do you have about this?

1._____
2._____
3._____

Who has your addiction affected?

1._____
2._____
3._____
4._____
5._____
6._____

What has your addiction cost the people you listed above?

1. _____

2. _____

3. _____

4. _____

How do you feel about your sexual addiction costing others pain?

I feel _____

I feel _____

I feel _____

Why do you want to recover from your sexual addiction?

1. _____

2. _____

3. _____

4. _____

What do you hope to gain by completing Step One?

1. _____

2. _____

3. _____

Do you feel you were truthful while completing this step? Why or why not?

_____

_____

Could you build a new future from the work you have done during Step One? Why?

_____

_____

_____

_____

"We admitted we were powerless over our sexual addiction and that our lives had become unmanageable." When and where do you feel you fully experienced Step One? (Give a specific place and time). If you are unable to identify a particular place and time when you experienced your Step One, what makes you believe you completed it?

_____
_____
_____
_____

What is the most significant thing you have learned about yourself during Step One?

_____
_____
_____
_____

On a scale from 1-10, rate yourself on the work you did in Step One.

1   2   3   4   5   6   7   8   9   10

Why?_____
_____

FEEDBACK FORM

The following space is provided for feedback from your group on your Step work. Use this feedback page for reflection or for continued work on your Step One. May your future journey of recovery begin with this first step.

Name of Group Member _____ Rating 1 2 3 4 5 6 7 8 9 10

Feedback _____

_____

_____

Name of Group Member _____ Rating 1 2 3 4 5 6 7 8 9 10

Feedback _____

_____

_____

Name of Group Member _____ Rating 1 2 3 4 5 6 7 8 9 10

Feedback _____

_____

_____

Name of Group Member _____ Rating 1 2 3 4 5 6 7 8 9 10

Feedback _____

_____

_____

Name of Group Member _____ Rating 1 2 3 4 5 6 7 8 9 10

Feedback _____

_____

_____

Name of Group Member _____ Rating 1 2 3 4 5 6 7 8 9 10

Feedback _____

_____

_____

"Came to believe that a Power greater than ourselves could restore us to sanity."

⇒ CAME

The verb came in Step Two is in the past tense. This word implies the action has already happened. This means that in this step we are reporting a past event. Highlight some examples of God's grace and how he revealed Himself to you when you became a believer in Jesus Christ as your Lord and Savior. (i.e., Being witnessed to, exposed to Christian events, etc.)

1. _____
2. _____
3. _____
4. _____
5. _____
6. _____
7. _____
8. _____
9. _____
10. _____

⇒ BELIEVE

Change in beliefs produces growth and change in behaviors. What areas of personal growth have occurred in you since you came to believe in Jesus Christ as your Lord and Savior?

1. _____

2._____

3._____

4._____

⇒ A POWER GREATER

The phrase A Power Greater was the only change of wording in the Twelve Steps from its original writing. The first writing of the Twelve Steps, which began in an Oxford Bible Study and which birthed AA, read "God" instead of "A Power Greater." The change was made because of the stigma that alcoholics had in the 1930's. To be an alcoholic was very shaming at this time in history. For the alcoholic to go to "God" with his shame was very difficult, so the writers of the Twelve Steps made the phrase A Power Greater instead, to give the alcoholic a little time to develop a God concept. The support groups allow God to patiently reveal Himself to them. Christians can begin to use Christ in their recovery. Bringing Jesus Christ into your recovery is also a process.

Give specific examples of coming to a point of belief in Jesus in different areas of your life.

1._____

2._____

3._____

What were the results of your faith in these areas of your life?

1._____

2._____

3._____

How has your coming to Christ affected your attitudes?

_____

_____

How has your coming to believe in Jesus Christ affected your behavior in the past and present?

1._____

2._____

3._____

How has your coming to believe in Jesus Christ affected your relationships in the past or present with those listed below.

Yourself

1._____

2._____

3. _____

Spouse

1. _____
2. _____
3. _____

Children

1. _____
2. _____
3. _____

Parents

1. _____
2. _____
3. _____

Work Relationships

1. _____
2. _____
3. _____

When did you come to believe in Jesus Christ? (Approximate date)

_____

What happened exactly?

_____

_____

_____

How would you define "greater"?

_____

_____

How do you understand the word or concept of power?

___

What are the powers that are greater than yourself? Why?

1. ___
2. ___
3. ___

What characteristics of Jesus Christ do you believe in?

1. ___
2. ___
3. ___
4. ___
5. ___

How do you know you can believe in Jesus Christ? Be specific as to how He has revealed His power to you.

1. ___
2. ___
3. ___
4. ___
5. ___
6. ___

How do you intend to utilize this relationship with Jesus Christ in your recovery from sexual addiction?

___

If you had this relationship in the past, what led you away from Him?

___

How long have you been away from your relationship with Jesus Christ?

_____

_____

_____

How did you feel about being apart from Him?

1. I felt _____

Explain how you have experienced Jesus Christ to be greater than all of yourself since you have chosen recovery?

1._____

2._____

3._____

Describe your current relationship with Jesus Christ. _____

_____

_____

What activities or behaviors are involved in your relationship with Him?

1._____

2._____

3._____

4._____

5._____

6._____

How much time in a day or a week do you invest in your relationship with Jesus Christ?

In a Day _____ In a Week _____

⇒ COULD

What does it mean to you to believe that Jesus Christ could do something to influence your recovery?

_____

_____

In what ways do you see Jesus Christ becoming involved in your sexual addiction recovery?

1._____
2._____
3._____
4._____

➡ RESTORE

What does the word restore mean to you?_____
_____

In what ways would Jesus have to restore you in the following areas of your life?

Spiritually_____
_____
_____

Fun/Recreation/Entertainment_____
_____
_____

Parenting_____
_____
_____

Financially_____
_____
_____

Sexually_____
_____
_____

Friendships_____
_____
_____

Relationship with yourself _____
_____
_____

Your Future _____
_____
_____

Marriage _____
_____
_____

What do you hope to gain by completing Step Two?

1. _____
2. _____
3. _____

Do you feel you were truthful while completing this step? Why or why not?

_____
_____

Could you build a new future from the work you have done? Why?

_____
_____

"Came to believe that a Power greater than ourselves could restore us to sanity." Do you feel you have fully experienced Step Two? Why or why not?

_____
_____
_____
_____

What is the most significant thing you have learned about yourself during Step Two?

_____
_____
_____
_____

On a scale from 1-10, rate yourself on the work you did in Step Two.

1 2 3 4 5 6 7 8 9 10

Why? _____
_____

FEEDBACK FORM

The following space is provided for feedback from your group on your Step work. Use this feedback page for reflection or for continued work on your Step One. May your future journey of recovery begin with this first step.

Name of Group Member _____ Rating 1 2 3 4 5 6 7 8 9 10

Feedback _____

_____

_____

Name of Group Member _____ Rating 1 2 3 4 5 6 7 8 9 10

Feedback _____

_____

_____

Name of Group Member _____ Rating 1 2 3 4 5 6 7 8 9 10

Feedback _____

_____

_____

Name of Group Member _____ Rating 1 2 3 4 5 6 7 8 9 10

Feedback _____

_____

_____

Name of Group Member _____ Rating 1 2 3 4 5 6 7 8 9 10

Feedback _____

_____

_____

Name of Group Member _____ Rating 1 2 3 4 5 6 7 8 9 10

Feedback _____

_____

_____

"Made a decision to turn our will and our lives over to the care of God as we understood Him."

⇒ MADE

Made is the past tense of the verb "to make." Make can be defined as a process involving effort to build or construct something. There are processes which are involved in making a decision. What are some of the events that have brought you to the point of deciding to turn your life and will over to God?

1. _____
2. _____
3. _____

As a sex addict, you have turned your will and life over to various things, persons or beliefs. List the things, persons or beliefs to which you had turned over your will and life over to in the past. Be specific.

1. _____
2. _____
3. _____
4. _____

Have you made decisions in the past to turn your life over to God? (i.e., "If you get me out of this one...") List them.

1. _____
2. _____
3. _____

Have you had moments of desperation, whether while acting-out or in recovery, when you cried out to God to take control over your life? (i.e., Praying after acting-out) List them.

1. _____
2. _____
3. _____
4. _____

How is this decision different today from those in the past? _____
_____
_____
_____

Since the word made is in the past tense, explain how you have been affected since turning your will and life over to the care of God, especially in your sexual addiction. What has changed? What are you doing differently?

1. _____
2. _____
3. _____
4. _____

Making a major decision in your life often requires time and a lot of thought. What were other major decisions you made in the past? How long did it take to make them? (Marriage/divorce/business choices)

1. _____
2. _____
3. _____
4. _____

In the previous cases, where were you (spiritually and/or emotionally) when you made that final decision?

1. _____
2. _____
3. _____
4. _____

If Step Three is thought through carefully, it is probably a decision much like marriage or choosing a vocation. How much time have you put into this step up to this point?

_____

_____

Can you identify a specific moment or culminating event that marks when you initially made the decision to turn your life and your will over to God in your recovery from sexual addiction?

If so, please explain.

_____

_____

_____

_____

If the previous answer is no, explain how you know you have completed your Step Three.

_____

_____

What areas in your life are you most reluctant to have God in charge?

List the areas	Why?
1. _____	1. _____
2. _____	2. _____
3. _____	3. _____
4. _____	4. _____

Explain how you will allow God to have His will in these areas.

1. _____

2. _____

3. _____

4. _____

5. _____

Over what specific sexual behaviors in your life do you want God to be in charge?

1. _____ 3. _____

2. _____ 4. _____

How do you intend to give Him charge over these sexual behaviors?

1. _____
2. _____
3. _____
4. _____

How are you turning your will to act out in these sexual manners over to God?

_____
_____
_____
_____

When did you turn over your will to God, and how have you been behaving differently since?

_____
_____
_____
_____

➡ CARE

What other words come to mind when you hear the word care as it pertains to the "care of God"?

1. _____   3. _____
2. _____   4. _____

How has God cared for you since you have given your will and life to Him?

1. _____
2. _____
3. _____

Has God demonstrated His care for you before you made this decision? If so, list three times.

1. _____
2. _____
3. _____

➡ GOD

The idea of God can be scary to those in recovery from sexual addiction. Explain God as you understand Him.

_____
_____
_____
_____
_____
_____
_____

What are characteristics you like and dislike about God?

Like?	Dislike?
1.	1.
2.	2.
3.	3.
4.	4.
5.	5.

Does God have the freedom to be the final authority in the areas listed below?

Socially	Yes	No	Job	Yes	No
Financially	Yes	No	Parenting	Yes	No
Marriage	Yes	No	Recovery	Yes	No
Dating	Yes	No	Spiritually	Yes	No
Sexually	Yes	No	Other Addictions	Yes	No

Why do you trust God with your will and life? _____
_____
_____

What do you consider to be your will? _____

_____

_____

What do you consider to be your life? _____

_____

What percentage are you turning over and why? Will _____% Life _____%

_____

⇒ AS WE UNDERSTAND HIM

We can all learn more about God through prayer, reading the Bible, regular church involvement and support groups. Ask four people who have been in recovery for longer than you to describe "God as they understand Him," as He is active in their lives now. Record their responses.

1. _____
2. _____
3. _____
4. _____

How do you presently practice learning more about God?

1. _____
2. _____
3. _____
4. _____

List behaviors or events that demonstrate you have turned your will over to God instead of allowing self-will to do as it pleases.

1. _____
2. _____
3. _____
4. _____

In what way have you turned your life over to God in these areas?

Family_____

_____

Spouse or Dating _____

_____

Sexually _____

_____

Job _____

_____

Future _____

_____

Financially _____

_____

Recovery _____

_____

Socially _____

_____

Write a letter to God turning your life and will over to Him.

Dear God,

"Made a decision to turn our will and our lives over to the care of God as we understood Him." Do you feel you have fully experienced Step Three? Why or why not?

_____
_____
_____
_____

What is the most significant thing you have learned about yourself during Step Three?

_____
_____
_____
_____

On a scale from 1-10, rate yourself on the work you did in Step Three.

1 2 3 4 5 6 7 8 9 10

Why? _____
_____

FEEDBACK FORM

The following space is provided for feedback from your group on your Step work. Use this feedback page for reflection or for continued work on your Step One. May your future journey of recovery begin with this first step.

Name of Group Member _____ Rating 1 2 3 4 5 6 7 8 9 10

Feedback _____

_____

_____

Name of Group Member _____ Rating 1 2 3 4 5 6 7 8 9 10

Feedback _____

_____

_____

Name of Group Member _____ Rating 1 2 3 4 5 6 7 8 9 10

Feedback _____

_____

_____

Name of Group Member _____ Rating 1 2 3 4 5 6 7 8 9 10

Feedback _____

_____

_____

Name of Group Member _____ Rating 1 2 3 4 5 6 7 8 9 10

Feedback _____

_____

_____

Name of Group Member _____ Rating 1 2 3 4 5 6 7 8 9 10

Feedback _____

_____

_____

"Made a searching and fearless moral inventory of ourselves."

⇒ MADE

By the end of Step Four, we will have made (past tense) a moral inventory of ourselves. Many sex addicts, in the midst of their addiction, did not have the clarity of mind to distinguish between moral or immoral behavior. It is now necessary to do so, lest the guilt or grandiosity pulls you back into your addiction. List strengths and weaknesses you have in the following areas of your life.

List strengths and weaknesses you have in the spiritual areas of your life.

Strengths   Weaknesses

1. _____   1. _____
2. _____   2. _____
3. _____   3. _____
4. _____   4. _____

List strengths and weaknesses you have in the financial areas of your life.

Strengths   Weaknesses

1. _____   1. _____
2. _____   2. _____
3. _____   3. _____
4. _____   4. _____

List strengths and weaknesses you have in your relationships.

Strengths

1. _____
2. _____
3. _____
4. _____

Weaknesses

1. _____
2. _____
3. _____
4. _____

List strengths and weaknesses you have in your marital relationship.

Strengths

1. _____
2. _____
3. _____
4. _____

Weaknesses

1. _____
2. _____
3. _____
4. _____

List strengths and weaknesses you have in your vocation.

Strengths

1. _____
2. _____
3. _____
4. _____

Weaknesses

1. _____
2. _____
3. _____
4. _____

List strengths and weaknesses you have had in relating to your Mother.

Strengths

1. _____
2. _____
3. _____
4. _____

Weaknesses

1. _____
2. _____
3. _____
4. _____

List strengths and weaknesses you have had in relating to your Father.

Strengths

1. _____
2. _____
3. _____
4. _____

Weaknesses

1. _____
2. _____
3. _____
4. _____

List strengths and weaknesses you have had in <u>relating to your Siblings</u>.

Strengths	Weaknesses
1. _____	1. _____
2. _____	2. _____
3. _____	3. _____
4. _____	4. _____

List strengths and weaknesses you have had in <u>relating to Yourself</u>.

Strengths	Weaknesses
1. _____	1. _____
2. _____	2. _____
3. _____	3. _____
4. _____	4. _____

List strengths and weaknesses you have had in <u>relating sexually with your spouse</u>.

Strengths	Weaknesses
1. _____	1. _____
2. _____	2. _____
3. _____	3. _____
4. _____	4. _____

List strengths and weaknesses you have had in <u>relating to Authorities</u>.

Strengths	Weaknesses
1. _____	1. _____
2. _____	2. _____
3. _____	3. _____
4. _____	4. _____

The above assessment gives an idea of how positive or negative your behaviors have been toward yourself and others. There is yet another inventory to fearlessly take in this step. This inventory is a deliberate search for additional moral information about yourself. You will need to be alert as you look at strengths, shortcomings or losses you have had up to this point in your life. These losses may not have been intentional but have nevertheless caused losses toward others. You may have suffered a loss of innocence by being sexually abused or sexually abusing others.

⇒ LOSSES

Inventory your losses in the left column, including harm that was done to you or harm that you may have caused toward others. This could include physical, sexual, emotional abuse; divorce; affairs; death of a loved one; losses could include being adopted or abandoned by a parent; school or legal issues, sexual activity, and other significant events.

⇒ STRENGTHS

In the right column, list positive events such as school events, career advancements, marriage, and the birth of children. Be specific. Include what happened, with whom, as well as your feelings then and now about the event.

Ages 1-5

Losses

Strengths

Ages 6-10

Losses

Strengths

Ages 11-15

Losses

Strengths

Ages 16-25

Losses

Strengths

Age 26-35

Losses

Strengths

Ages 36-45

Losses

Strengths

Ages 46-55

Losses

Strengths

Ages 56+

Losses

Strengths

Have you been 100% honest in writing down the losses that you are aware of?

Yes _____ No _____

Are there specific things you were too ashamed to write down at this point in your recovery?

Yes _____ No _____

Have you been sexually abused by a male?

Yes _____ No _____

Did you include this in your inventory?

Yes _____ No _____

Were you sexually abused by a female older than yourself when you were a child?

Yes _____ No _____

Describe your first sexual encounter. _____
_____
_____

⇒ OURSELVES

The recovering community can help us learn much about ourselves. Contact four recovering people who have completed Step Four and ask them what they learned about themselves during this step. Record their first name and answers in the space provided below.

1. _____
2. _____
3. _____
4. _____

What have you learned in this step about the word ourselves?

1. _____
2. _____
3. _____
4. _____

What specifically have you learned about yourself?

1. _____
2. _____

"Made a searching and fearless moral inventory of ourselves." Do you feel you have fully experienced Step Four? Why or why not?

___

What is the most significant thing you have learned about yourself during Step Four?

___

On a scale from 1-10, rate yourself on the work you did in Step Four.

1 2 3 4 5 6 7 8 9 10

Why? ___

FEEDBACK FORM

The following space is provided for feedback from your group on your Step work. Use this feedback page for reflection or for continued work on your Step One. May your future journey of recovery begin with this first step.

Name of Group Member _____ Rating 1 2 3 4 5 6 7 8 9 10

Feedback _____
_____
_____

Name of Group Member _____ Rating 1 2 3 4 5 6 7 8 9 10

Feedback _____
_____
_____

Name of Group Member _____ Rating 1 2 3 4 5 6 7 8 9 10

Feedback _____
_____
_____

Name of Group Member _____ Rating 1 2 3 4 5 6 7 8 9 10

Feedback _____
_____
_____

Name of Group Member _____ Rating 1 2 3 4 5 6 7 8 9 10

Feedback _____
_____
_____

Name of Group Member _____ Rating 1 2 3 4 5 6 7 8 9 10

Feedback _____
_____
_____

"Admitted to God, to ourselves, and to another human being the exact nature of our wrongs."

So far in your journey, you have been either reunited with or introduced to Jesus for the first time. Knowing Him will help you to admit to Him the exact nature of your wrongs. The journey through Step Four gave you some awareness of yourself. Step Five will further aid you in this understanding.

➡ ADMITTING

Admitting can often be the hardest thing to do. Are there reasons you don't want to entirely admit the exact nature of your wrongs? (i.e., fear of being rejected if others knew, or if the behavior was against the law?) List these.

1._____

2._____

3._____

If you listed any reasons, get feedback from a few recovering people who have already gone through Step Five. How did they deal with these issues?

1._____

2._____

3._____

Ask four recovering people who have done their Step Five what some of their experiences were in doing this step.

1._____

2._____

3._____

Ask these same people what feelings they had after doing their Step Five.

1._____

2._____

3._____

It is time for you to do some reckoning. Often, to our own harm as sex addicts, we continuously carry a list of things we have done wrong. It is time to write this list on paper. Make a list of people you are aware of that you have wronged and their relationship to you. Record the wrong done to each person. Use additional paper if necessary.

Name & Relationship	Wrong Done

Now that you have looked at your wrongs from a relational point of view, it is time to look at them chronologically. On the following pages, in chronological order, write the names of those you have wronged physically, sexually, emotionally, etc. Use your Step Four to help you in this process.

In the space provided list names of people wronged and a brief explanation of the exact wrong. Include those on previous pages.

Age 1-5

Ages 6-10

Ages 11-15

Ages 16 - 25

Ages 26 - 35

Ages 36-45

Ages 46 - 55

Ages 46 - 55

Ages 56-65

Ages 66+

After acknowledging the exact nature of our wrongs, we need to admit them to another human being of the same sex. What type of person do you feel this person we admit to should be?

1._____

2._____

3._____

Do you have someone picked out? If not, why not? _____

_____

_____

If so, what is the person's first name and relationship to you? _____

When did you verbally communicate all the information you wrote down in this step to someone of the same sex?

Date _____

Did you hold anything back that you were too embarrassed to tell?

Yes _____ No _____

If you answered yes, list the things you withheld and make a second appointment with this person to finish this step. Freedom requires 100% honesty.

1._____

2._____

3._____

How do you feel about completing this step?

I feel _____

I feel _____

How do you feel about yourself?

I feel _____

I feel _____

"Admitted to God, to ourselves, and to another human being the exact nature of our wrongs." Do you feel you have fully experienced Step Five? Why or why not?

_____
_____
_____
_____

What is the most significant thing you have learned about yourself during Step Five?

_____
_____
_____
_____

On a scale from 1-10, rate yourself on the work you did in Step Five.

1 2 3 4 5 6 7 8 9 10

Why?_____
_____

FEEDBACK FORM

The following space is provided for feedback from your group on your Step work. Use this feedback page for reflection or for continued work on your Step One. May your future journey of recovery begin with this first step.

Name of Group Member _____ Rating 1 2 3 4 5 6 7 8 9 10

Feedback _____
_____
_____

Name of Group Member _____ Rating 1 2 3 4 5 6 7 8 9 10

Feedback _____
_____
_____

Name of Group Member _____ Rating 1 2 3 4 5 6 7 8 9 10

Feedback _____
_____
_____

Name of Group Member _____ Rating 1 2 3 4 5 6 7 8 9 10

Feedback _____
_____
_____

Name of Group Member _____ Rating 1 2 3 4 5 6 7 8 9 10

Feedback _____
_____
_____

Name of Group Member _____ Rating 1 2 3 4 5 6 7 8 9 10

Feedback _____
_____
_____

"Were entirely ready to have God remove all these defects of character."

➡ ENTIRELY

When we think of the word entirely, many pictures come to mind. One of the most vivid pictures is that of a sprinter with his foot on the block and hands in the dirt in front of the white line, anticipating the sound of the gun going off. He is entirely ready. This is an appropriate picture for entirely. Entirely is 100% ready to do something. Many addicts in the midst of their addiction have been entirely ready to destroy themselves for the high, the fix, the relationship, or the avoidance of pain from the past.

Now you have come to another point in your life where you need to be entirely ready, after completing Steps One through Five, to do something to better yourself.

What are some of the words you think of when you think of the word entirely?

1._____

2._____

3._____

What are some of the feelings you have when you think of the word entirely?

I feel _____

I feel _____

What are a couple of examples in your life when you were entirely ready to do something? (Be specific.)

_____

_____

_____

➡ TO HAVE GOD (JESUS)

Who has Jesus become to you during your journey through Steps One through Five?

___

What roles is He filling in your life?

___

What feelings do you have towards Jesus at this point?

___

Why do you think that we need to have God involved in this part of the recovery process?

___

How have you relied upon Jesus in the past?

___

What aspects or characteristics of God are you relying upon to help in the process of removing your defects of character?

___

➡ REMOVE

Remove is another word in recovery that can mean something very painful for a sex addict. Remove in the form of an analogy can mean "to remove weeds from your grass by pulling them up". Another picture could be to remove a tumor that in the future could kill you.

What are some words or phrases you think of when you think of the word remove?

1. ___
2. ___

3._____

4._____

What are some of the feelings you have when you think of something being removed from you?

I feel _____

I feel _____

What are some of the things that have been removed from you up to this point in your sexual addiction recovery?

1._____

2._____

3._____

How do you feel about these things being removed?

_____

_____

How has God been involved in the removal process?

_____

_____

➡ ALL

All means quite a bit to anyone in recovery. It is going to mean a lot in Step Six, as well. What words or phrases come to your mind when you think of the word all?

1._____

2._____

3._____

What percentage is all? _____%

What percentage do you want all to mean when you talk about removing your defects of character?

_____%

➡ DEFECTS

Defects are shortcomings or flaws. It doesn't mean we are any less lovable or less human. A diamond, no matter how valuable, large, or beautiful it is, has carbon spots in it somewhere. All people have carbon spots. This is part of being human. This is not something to be ashamed about, nor is it something to be proud of; it is, however, something we can accept - and at this point - identify in ourselves.

What are some of the defects that you have seen in your past?

Ages 1-10

1. _____
2. _____
3. _____
4. _____
5. _____

Ages 11 - 20

1. _____
2. _____
3. _____
4. _____
5. _____

Ages 21 - 30

1. _____
2. _____
3. _____
4. _____
5. _____

Ages 41 - 50

1. _____
2. _____
3. _____
4. _____
5. _____

Ages 51+

1. _____
2. _____

3. _____

4. _____

5. _____

What are some of the defects you have in relating to the following people or areas of your life?

Yourself

1. _____

2. _____

3. _____

Your family of origin

1. _____

2. _____

3. _____

Your spouse

1. _____

2. _____

3. _____

Your children

1. _____

2. _____

3. _____

Your employer

1. _____

2. _____

3. _____

Your spiritual authorities

1. _____

2. _____

3. _____

Your friends

1. _____
2. _____
3. _____

Your Lord

1. _____
2. _____
3. _____

Compile a full list of these defects of character, the length of time you have been aware of their existence, and the percentage at this point that you are willing to have them removed. An example is given below.

Example: Defects	Length of Time	Percentage
Self willed	32 years	80-90%

DEFECTS	LENGTH OF TIME	PERCENTAGE

Take time to write about each character defect and on separate paper, write a paragraph about each one and what life would be like without that defect in your life. Use the following lines to summarize your writings when you have finished.

_____
_____
_____
_____
_____
_____
_____
_____
_____
_____
_____
_____

Write the character defects that you are 100% ready to have God remove. Only write those you are totally ready to have God remove. In other words, if God could take the defect from you, you would let Him have them and not want to take them back.

_____   _____
_____   _____
_____   _____
_____   _____

If you are not ready to have all of your defects removed, have a daily time of prayer and meditation, until you are entirely ready to let God remove them all. Write the date below that you became entirely ready for Him to remove all the defects.

_____/_____/_____

➡ CHARACTER

Character is what you are as a person. As mentioned earlier, there are carbon spots in every person and these spots are important for you to identify. If you know where the spots are, you can surely ask God to help you with them.

This ends your journey through Step Six. Step Six simply asks you to become entirely ready to have God remove all your defects of character. You have listed your defects and thought through what it would be like to have them removed.

"Were entirely ready to have God remove all these defects of character." Do you feel you have fully experienced Step Six? Why or why not?

_____

_____

_____

_____

What is the most significant thing you have learned about yourself during Step Six?

_____

_____

_____

_____

On a scale from 1-10, rate yourself on the work you did in Step Six.

1 2 3 4 5 6 7 8 9 10

Why?_____

_____

FEEDBACK FORM

The following space is provided for feedback from your group on your Step work. Use this feedback page for reflection or for continued work on your Step One. May your future journey of recovery begin with this first step.

Name of Group Member _____ Rating 1 2 3 4 5 6 7 8 9 10

Feedback _____

_____

_____

Name of Group Member _____ Rating 1 2 3 4 5 6 7 8 9 10

Feedback _____

_____

_____

Name of Group Member _____ Rating 1 2 3 4 5 6 7 8 9 10

Feedback _____

_____

_____

Name of Group Member _____ Rating 1 2 3 4 5 6 7 8 9 10

Feedback _____

_____

_____

Name of Group Member _____ Rating 1 2 3 4 5 6 7 8 9 10

Feedback _____

_____

_____

Name of Group Member _____ Rating 1 2 3 4 5 6 7 8 9 10

Feedback _____

_____

_____

"Humbly asked Him to remove our shortcomings."

➡ HUMBLY

Humbly can be defined as a disposition, an attitude, a reverence, or a submissiveness. I can remember a couple of instances during my school years when I was called into the principal's office and felt humble while waiting to go into his office, because I knew the principal could impact my life. An authority figure can have an effect on me; he had the authority to do something, either positively or negatively, and I was at his mercy. This feeling of humbleness was likely also experienced in your life. Many have experienced something similar to this in their lives at some point. The scriptures are very clear about the virtue of humbleness in Colossians 3:12, James 4:7-10, and I Peter 5:5-6.

What are some of the experiences you have had that have caused you to feel humble?

1._____
2._____
3._____

What are the feelings that accompanied you in those experiences when you were humbled?

I felt _____

I felt _____

When was the last time you were in an experience like that?

_____

➡ ASKED

A quote from the Bible - James 4:2 - says "You have not because you ask not." This is also true as it relates to our recovery in Step Seven. Many sex addicts have never honestly or fully looked at their character defects or limitations. On the following pages, we will search further in the meaning of asked, now that you have an intelligent, prepared list to ask from.

What are some of the things that you have asked of God and received them?

1._____
2._____
3._____

Many times it takes "faith," "trust," or even "hope" in asking. Some have felt or feel desperate and full of despair because of shortcomings in their past or current life and felt/feel as if there is no way out. Now you come to a point where you can ask. Asking doesn't always mean it is going to happen the way you want it to, or that you are going to be in control of the procedure. But let's look at the possibility of asking.

What are some of the character defects you identified in Step Six that you would like to ask to be removed?

1._____
2._____
3._____
4._____
5._____
6._____
7._____
8._____
9._____
10._____

⇒ HIM

What are some of the aspects of God you are clinging to as you ask Him to do these things for you?

_____
_____

Have you experienced these characteristics of God before in your relationship with Him? If so, how?

1._____
2._____
3._____
4._____
5._____

⇒ REMOVE

We talked about the word remove in Step Six. This is where you ask for it to actually happen. You are beyond "entirely ready." You are at the physician's table asking Him to make an incision and remove the cancer and all the things that ails you. You are asking Him to cut deep into your mind and will and remove. During this surgical procedure, there are a variety of experiences that you may have.

What are some of the experiences you are anticipating to happen?

1._____

2._____

3._____

Have you had any experience with God removing anything else in your life?   Yes _____ No _____

If so, explain what and how he removed it.

_____

_____

Did you believe that He would do the removal the way He did?   Yes _____ No _____

It is true that the removal process is somewhat of a mystery. Who would think that to create patience you would experience situations that would cause you to become patient? Who would think that in the process of becoming kind, you would have to actually change or behave in a new way? Many of the processes which God is going to use in our life are not in our control, nor should they be. The removing is not our doing. It is clear that we are asking someone else to do something, much like asking a surgeon to fix something. We don't have the insight nor the education that these surgeons have, nor would many of us want it. We just have to trust that they can do what we are asking them to do.

Have you seen God remove things in other people's lives?   Yes _____ No _____

Was he successful in these surgeries?   Yes _____ No _____

What are some of the feelings you have about God being in control of removing the things that you have listed as being 100% ready to remove in Step Six?

I feel _____

I feel _____

⇒ OUR

The word Our is one of the great words of the Twelve Steps. It means that there is more than just one person who has gone through this. You are not alone, nor will you ever be.

Who are some of the people you know who have done their Step Seven?

1._____

2._____

3._____

4._____

What were some of their experiences after going through Step Seven? List These.

1._____

2._____

3._____

4._____

⇒ SHORTCOMINGS

Shortcomings are similar to defects. They are the carbon spots or issues identified in Step Six.

Review your Step Six and look carefully over the character defects you identified as being 100% ready to have God remove. Write out your prayers to God to remove one character defect at a time. Don't rob yourself and try to clump them all together. Ask Him to take His knowledge and ways to systematically remove them and give Him full permission to rank them in the order He sees most important and viable. It is much like surgery. Sometimes the surgeon has to prioritize what is going on within the system. If someone has been shot, the surgeon has to look past something else to get at what is primary. Allow God to prioritize as He removes these aspects.

In the following spaces, write the list of defects & the date you prayed for removal. come back to this in one year, and see how much work God has done.

DEFECTS	DATE PRAYED FOR REMOVAL	MY ONE YEAR PROGRESS NOTE

"Humbly asked Him to remove our shortcomings." Do you feel you have fully experienced Step Seven? Why or why not?

___

What is the most significant thing you've learned about yourself while completing Step Seven?

___

On a scale from 1-10, rate yourself on the work you did in Step Seven.

1 2 3 4 5 6 7 8 9 10

Why?___

FEEDBACK FORM

The following space is provided for feedback from your group on your Step work. Use this feedback page for reflection or for continued work on your Step One. May your future journey of recovery begin with this first step.

Name of Group Member _____ Rating 1 2 3 4 5 6 7 8 9 10

Feedback _____

_____

_____

Name of Group Member _____ Rating 1 2 3 4 5 6 7 8 9 10

Feedback _____

_____

_____

Name of Group Member _____ Rating 1 2 3 4 5 6 7 8 9 10

Feedback _____

_____

_____

Name of Group Member _____ Rating 1 2 3 4 5 6 7 8 9 10

Feedback _____

_____

_____

Name of Group Member _____ Rating 1 2 3 4 5 6 7 8 9 10

Feedback _____

_____

_____

Name of Group Member _____ Rating 1 2 3 4 5 6 7 8 9 10

Feedback _____

_____

_____

STEP 8

"Made a list of all people we had harmed, and became willing to make amends to them all."

➡ MADE A LIST

Thus far throughout the 12 Steps, we have made a decision to turn our life over to the care of God and made a searching and fearless inventory. Now you will take time, energy, and creativity to make a list.

➡ OF ALL PEOPLE

Again, we are confronted with the word all. All means 100% in this case. This includes people in your past and present that you may have victimized or hurt through your own addiction issues.

➡ WE

Again. it is very comforting to see the word We, confirming that you are not the only person who may have caused harm to others because of your addiction issues. Harm is a difficult word for many sex addicts and that is why it is here in Step Eight that you will address this. If you would have done this step earlier, you probably would not have been sober enough to realize that your attitudes and behaviors actually inflicted pain, whether knowingly or unknowingly. You may have caused many people whom you have known, loved, and deeply cared about a tremendous amount of shame or hurt. It is now time to look at the harm you have done to others while in your addiction.

Let's take a sober moment and consider prayer, asking God to help you to make this list. We will make this list chronological in order. This is similar to your list in Step Four. Now would be a good time to go back to Step Four and review the things you have done and the people you have hurt. Make a list of these people. Use additional paper if necessary.

Ages 1-12

Ages 13-20

Ages 21-30

Ages 31-40

Ages 41-50

Ages 51+

_____ _____
_____ _____
_____ _____
_____ _____
_____ _____

Take time to compile a list of people you may have caused pain to more than once.

_____ _____
_____ _____
_____ _____
_____ _____
_____ _____
_____ _____
_____ _____
_____ _____
_____ _____

⇒ AND

And is a great conjunction. I am glad that you didn't stop at just making this list. If you did, it would be possibly too painful to bear.

How do you feel about making your list?

I feel _____

I feel _____

⇒ BECAME

This is a process. It takes time. Give yourself permission to become willing to make amends. This is similar to Step Four and Five where you are reckoning a part of yourself. How did you feel after you completed Step Five?

I felt _____

I felt _____

⇒ WILLING

We have talked about the word willing indirectly in Step Six when we discussed being "entirely ready." Willing means that you are, regardless of emotion, willing to submit or comply to what needs to be done. This doesn't mean that you are going to do it yet, just that you are willing. For those who exercise, it is similar to lying in bed and at some point become willing to get up and then move into the direction of going to exercise. You don't just arrive at the gym immediately but begin moving in that direction.

What are some experiences you have had in becoming willing during your recovery?

1._____
2._____
3._____

What were the results of this willingness?

1._____
2._____
3._____

⇒ MAKE AMENDS

An amend is making something right again, to restore or try to mend something that has been broken. Many of us will do this as we move from our Step Eight to our Step Nine. Part of Step Eight is that we become willing to make that step and mend what has been broken and acknowledge our responsibility in the breaking of it.

⇒ TO THEM ALL

What percentage is all? _____%

Make a list of these people again & indicate the % of your willingness to make amends to each one.

1._____ _____%   11._____ _____%
2._____ _____%   12._____ _____%
3._____ _____%   13._____ _____%
4._____ _____%   14._____ _____%
5._____ _____%   15._____ _____%
6._____ _____%   16._____ _____%
7._____ _____%   17._____ _____%
8._____ _____%   18._____ _____%
9._____ _____%   19._____ _____%
10._____ _____%   20._____ _____%

Use this list, praying regularly, until you become 100% willing to make amends to them all. Some people in recovery stay at Step Eight for some time until they become willing to make amends to them all. There are some experiences that are quite painful. Step Eight is to get us to the point where we are willing. Below write the date when you became 100% willing to make amends to every person on this list.

_____

"Made a lite of all people we had harmed, and became willing to make amends to them all." Do you feel you have fully experienced Step Eight? Why or why not?

_____
_____
_____
_____

What is the most significant thing you have learned about yourself during Step Eight?

_____
_____
_____
_____

On a scale from 1 to 10, rate yourself on Step Eight.

1 2 3 4 5 6 7 8 9 10

Why?_____
_____

FEEDBACK FORM

The following space is provided for feedback from your group on your Step work. Use this feedback page for reflection or for continued work on your Step One. May your future journey of recovery begin with this first step.

Name of Group Member _____ Rating 1 2 3 4 5 6 7 8 9 10

Feedback _____

_____

_____

Name of Group Member _____ Rating 1 2 3 4 5 6 7 8 9 10

Feedback _____

_____

_____

Name of Group Member _____ Rating 1 2 3 4 5 6 7 8 9 10

Feedback _____

_____

_____

Name of Group Member _____ Rating 1 2 3 4 5 6 7 8 9 10

Feedback _____

_____

_____

Name of Group Member _____ Rating 1 2 3 4 5 6 7 8 9 10

Feedback _____

_____

_____

Name of Group Member _____ Rating 1 2 3 4 5 6 7 8 9 10

Feedback _____

_____

_____

STEP 9

"Made direct amends to such people wherever possible,
except when to do so would injure them or others."

➡ MADE

This is the last time the word made is used in your Twelve Step journey and it may also be the most painful. Now you will turn your energies, creativity, and time into making direct amends to those we have harmed.

➡ DIRECT

What are some words you think of when you hear the word direct?

1._____

2._____

3._____

What are some words that come to mind that are opposite of direct?

1._____

2._____

3._____

How do you feel about these opposite words when someone is behaving that way toward you?

I feel _____

I feel _____

How do you feel about someone who is being direct toward you?

I feel _____

I feel _____

Direct is the straightest line between any two points. In the past, most sex addicts have been vague, shamed and blamed others, and have avoided and rationalized many behaviors. Some of your own defense mechanisms were to blame others for your behavior. You also rationalized your behaviors, claiming you weren't responsible. In addition, you minimized your behaviors and were not able to see the damage done in other people's lives. These defense mechanisms helped you stay in sexual addiction, but they will not help you in recovery. Let's discuss what direct means.

The most to least direct amends methods in recovery are as follows:

1. Face to face contact: Talk to the person, face to face, and have a discussion regarding what you had done that caused them harm. This is the most direct amend that can be made in a relationship. This is by far the best method of being direct with your amends.

2. Phone calls: If the person is too far to travel to make a direct amend, then a phone call can suffice as a second most direct amend.

3. Letter: For the person who does not have a phone, or cannot be reached in any other manner, a letter is your least direct amend.

4. Symbolic: Symbolically put the person you are making an amend to in a chair facing you and make your amend to them. This would only be for people you don't know (such as one night stands, prostitutes) or other acting out partners. Do not use a symbolic amend for nonsexual offenses unless you first consult your sponsor or therapist.

➡ AMENDS

Making Amends is a process of fusing two pieces that are broken or at least bringing them into contact. You are not required to restore the relationship. An amend is only you cleaning your side of the street. It does not minimize, rationalize, or blame anyone for the behavior that caused pain. It is you looking fully at the pain that you caused another human being and acknowledging that pain to them. It is asking them to forgive you and advance in the relationship as they wish to. You are not responsible for their forgiveness. You are only 100% responsible for what you did to them. A word of caution - You may need the help of the group or a therapist to help you decide who you should or should not see. Going to see ex-lovers is not a good idea.

➡ SUCH PEOPLE

Make a list of the people from Step Eight and in the columns provided, check off the most direct method of amends you are able to do with each person.

NAME	FACE TO FACE	CALL	LETTER	SYMBOLIC
1. _____	_____	_____	_____	_____
2. _____	_____	_____	_____	_____
3. _____	_____	_____	_____	_____
4. _____	_____	_____	_____	_____
5. _____	_____	_____	_____	_____
6. _____	_____	_____	_____	_____
7. _____	_____	_____	_____	_____
8. _____	_____	_____	_____	_____
9. _____	_____	_____	_____	_____
10. _____	_____	_____	_____	_____
11. _____	_____	_____	_____	_____
12. _____	_____	_____	_____	_____
13. _____	_____	_____	_____	_____
14. _____	_____	_____	_____	_____
15. _____	_____	_____	_____	_____
16. _____	_____	_____	_____	_____
17. _____	_____	_____	_____	_____
18. _____	_____	_____	_____	_____
17. _____	_____	_____	_____	_____
18. _____	_____	_____	_____	_____
19. _____	_____	_____	_____	_____
20. _____	_____	_____	_____	_____

➡ WHENEVER POSSIBLE

In the 1930's when the steps were written, wherever possible was much more limited than today. Today, wherever possible is almost everywhere due to planes and technology that enables us to reach anyone in the world. Wherever possible is also acknowledging the fact that not everyone who you owe an amend to will be able to be reached, found or located. For this you are not responsible. If you are unable to locate someone, you are not responsible to make a direct amend. If you feel you need to make a symbolic amend, write them a letter and read it to them as if they were in a chair facing you. This may be helpful to your recovery and healing.

List those people who, after trying, you were unable to locate.

1._____
2._____
3._____
4._____
5._____

➡ EXCEPT

Except appears to be one of the bigger words to some addicts during this step. Many sex addicts say "Oh good, a loophole." However, this is not what the word except means. This word except is used very sparingly. It means that there are some on the list that need to be exceptions. List those that you currently believe would be exceptions because to do so would cause them or others injury or harm.

1._____
2._____
3._____
4._____
5._____

List five people you respect in recovery who have already done their Step Nine.

1._____
2._____
3._____
4._____
5._____

After talking to each of the persons you listed above, consider their perceptions of whether your list of exceptions are appropriate. After considering their feedback, list those left that continue to be exempt.

1._____
2._____
3._____
4._____
5._____

What is the injury or harm that would be caused if you made an amend to those on your above list?

1._____

2._____

3._____

4._____

5._____

After prayer and meditation, do you have peace about those not receiving a direct amend?

Yes _____ No _____

Make a list again of the people you owe amends to. In the column next to their name, list the date you made you amend, as you complete them. Caution: Do not wait but actively pursue this! Do this justice, however, and spend the necessary time preparing and making complete amends with each person. This step may take significant time to complete.

NAME   **DATE**

1. _____   _____
2. _____   _____
3. _____   _____
4. _____   _____
5. _____   _____
6. _____   _____
7. _____   _____
8. _____   _____
9. _____   _____
10. _____   _____
11. _____   _____
12. _____   _____
13. _____   _____
14. _____   _____
15. _____   _____
16. _____   _____
17. _____   _____
18. _____   _____
19. _____   _____
20. _____   _____

Complete your Step Nine by filling in the dates of all the amends made to the people on your list. Your Step Nine is not completed until the last date is listed.

How many direct amends can you make in the next week? Month? 3 Months?

1 Week _____   1 Month _____   3 Months _____

When you have completed making your amends, answer the following questions.

What were some of the experiences you had in doing your Step Nine? _____
_____
_____

What were some of your favorite conversations? _____

_____

_____

_____

_____

_____

_____

_____

_____

_____

_____

_____

_____

_____

What were some of the feelings you had before, during, and after making your amends?

Before, I felt _____

During, I felt _____

After, I felt _____

Now that you have made your amends, how do you feel about these relationships?

I feel _____

I feel _____

I feel _____

How do you feel about yourself now in the context of these relationships?

I feel _____

I feel _____

I feel _____

"Made direct amends to such people wherever possible, except when to do so would injure them or others." Do you feel you have fully experienced Step Nine? Why or why not?

_____
_____
_____
_____

What is the most significant thing you have learned about yourself during Step Nine?

_____
_____
_____
_____

On a scale from 1 to 10, rate yourself on Step Nine.

1 2 3 4 5 6 7 8 9 10

Why?_____
_____

FEEDBACK FORM

The following space is provided for feedback from your group on your Step work. Use this feedback page for reflection or for continued work on your Step One. May your future journey of recovery begin with this first step.

Name of Group Member _____ Rating 1 2 3 4 5 6 7 8 9 10

Feedback _____
_____
_____

Name of Group Member _____ Rating 1 2 3 4 5 6 7 8 9 10

Feedback _____
_____
_____

Name of Group Member _____ Rating 1 2 3 4 5 6 7 8 9 10

Feedback _____
_____
_____

Name of Group Member _____ Rating 1 2 3 4 5 6 7 8 9 10

Feedback _____
_____
_____

Name of Group Member _____ Rating 1 2 3 4 5 6 7 8 9 10

Feedback _____
_____
_____

Name of Group Member _____ Rating 1 2 3 4 5 6 7 8 9 10

Feedback _____
_____
_____

"Continued to take personal inventory and when we were wrong promptly admitted it."

⇒ CONTINUED

This is a process that will last a lifetime. Being human means making mistakes. Step Ten allows us to be human without accumulating guilt or shame from behavior or attitudes. Step Ten is a life-style. What is the date you are starting this life-style choice?

Date: _____

⇒ PERSONAL INVENTORY

A personal inventory is a recording of a person's behavior and attitudes. Behavior and attitudes can hurt us, as well as others. The other side of your inventory is strengths you have practiced today. Recovery will enable growth in your strengths. In Step Ten, don't proclaim your strengths to others. This is for you to know and to thank God for. In Step Ten, you are honest about your mistakes and then admit them to those you made the mistake toward.

Below is a form to use over the next month so that you can get into a healthy habit and also make sure that this principle is being applied regularly in your life. You are going to need to continue this behavior throughout your life. Now that you are shameless, you can relate to God more openly than ever before.

DAY	AMENDS ASKED FOR	STRENGTH ACKNOWLEDGED
1		
2		
3		
4		
5		
6		
7		
8		
9		
10		
11		
12		
13		
14		
15		
16		
17		
18		
19		
20		
21		
22		
23		
24		
25		
26		
27		
28		
29		
30		
31		

Your personal inventory is not up at the end of the month. This form is only used to get you into the habit of looking honestly at yourself without shame and help you to say "that was a mistake" and admit it promptly. Remember that being human means we all make mistakes; being mature means we admit them!

➡ PROMPTLY ADMITTED IT

Promptly means in a timely manner. It does not mean weeks or months later. It should not be much longer than the day you made the mistake. Admit it to yourself and the other person and move on. How long did it take you to make your amends after you were aware you needed to? (Write in the time it took in the blank space next to "Day ___")

Complete these questions after your 30 days of personal inventory is completed:

What is the average time you made an amend? _____

Does the above time fit your definition for prompt? Yes _____ No _____

If your answer is no, what is your plan to improve your promptness. Ask five people in the program that you know who have done their Step Ten and ask how they worked on promptness.

Record your findings below.

1. _____
2. _____
3. _____
4. _____
5. _____

"Continued to take personal inventory, and when we were wrong, promptly admitted it." Do you feel you have fully experienced Step Ten? Why or why not?

_____
_____
_____
_____

What is the most significant thing you have learned about yourself during Step Ten?

_____
_____
_____
_____

On a scale from 1 to 10, rate yourself on Step Ten.

1 2 3 4 5 6 7 8 9 10

Why?_____
_____

FEEDBACK FORM

The following space is provided for feedback from your group on your Step work. Use this feedback page for reflection or for continued work on your Step One. May your future journey of recovery begin with this first step.

Name of Group Member _____ Rating 1 2 3 4 5 6 7 8 9 10

Feedback _____
_____
_____

Name of Group Member _____ Rating 1 2 3 4 5 6 7 8 9 10

Feedback _____
_____
_____

Name of Group Member _____ Rating 1 2 3 4 5 6 7 8 9 10

Feedback _____
_____
_____

Name of Group Member _____ Rating 1 2 3 4 5 6 7 8 9 10

Feedback _____
_____
_____

Name of Group Member _____ Rating 1 2 3 4 5 6 7 8 9 10

Feedback _____
_____
_____

Name of Group Member _____ Rating 1 2 3 4 5 6 7 8 9 10

Feedback _____
_____
_____

STEP 11

"Sought through prayer and meditation to improve our conscious contact with God as we understood Him, praying only for the knowledge of His will for us and the power to carry that out."

➡ SOUGHT

The word sought means to seek with the intention to find. This takes time and effort. Do you put time aside to pray and meditate on a regular basis?

Yes _____ No _____

If your answer was no, start now. Set aside time to do this daily. Once this time is set, you may or may not want to involve another person to make sure that you are accountable. If you choose to do this, what is their name?

_____

Use the form included below to record your experiences during the next 31 days.

Day	Prayer	Meditation
1		
2		
3		
4		
5		
6		
7		
8		
9		
10		
11		
12		
13		
14		
15		
16		
17		
18		
19		
20		
21		
22		
23		
24		
25		
26		
27		
28		
29		
30		
31		

⇒ CONSCIOUS CONTACT

What have been some of your "conscious contact" experiences over the past thirty-one days?

_____
_____
_____

Some people journal their contacts with God. Would you like to make that a part of your spiritual life?

Yes _____ No _____

⇒ KNOWLEDGE OF HIS WILL

Other questions to ask yourself are "Am I praying for the knowledge of His will?" If you feel you are doing this, put a "Y" next to the days you are praying. As a Christian, this may already be a part of your life. In this step, it is a specific focus for recovery.

After you have completed the 31 days, answer the following questions:

What knowledge of His will have you gained over the past 31 days?

_____
_____
_____

In what ways has God given you the power to carry out His will as you have understood it during the past 31 days? Be specific.

_____
_____
_____

"Sought through prayer and meditation to improve our conscious contact with God as we understood Him, praying only for the knowledge of His will for us and the power to carry that out." Do you feel you have fully experienced Step Eleven? Why or why not?

_____
_____
_____

What is the most significant thing you learned about yourself in completing your Step Eleven?
_____
_____
_____
_____

On a scale from one to ten, rate yourself on Step Eleven.

1 2 3 4 5 6 7 8 9 10

Why?_____
_____

FEEDBACK FORM

The following space is provided for feedback from your group on your Step work. Use this feedback page for reflection or for continued work on your Step One. May your future journey of recovery begin with this first step.

Name of Group Member _____ Rating 1 2 3 4 5 6 7 8 9 10

Feedback _____

_____

_____

Name of Group Member _____ Rating 1 2 3 4 5 6 7 8 9 10

Feedback _____

_____

_____

Name of Group Member _____ Rating 1 2 3 4 5 6 7 8 9 10

Feedback _____

_____

_____

Name of Group Member _____ Rating 1 2 3 4 5 6 7 8 9 10

Feedback _____

_____

_____

Name of Group Member _____ Rating 1 2 3 4 5 6 7 8 9 10

Feedback _____

_____

_____

Name of Group Member _____ Rating 1 2 3 4 5 6 7 8 9 10

Feedback _____

_____

_____

STEP 12

"Having had a spiritual awakening as the result of these Steps, we tried to carry this message to others, and to practice these principles in all our affairs."

⟶ HAVING HAD A SPIRITUAL AWAKENING

In many ways recovery from sexual addiction has brought on several awakenings, all of which are spiritual. What were some of the awakenings that you have had in your spiritual life since you have started your sexual addiction recovery?

_____
_____
_____
_____
_____

What part of this awakening was a direct result of working the steps? _____

_____
_____

What steps seemed to be more important to you as a spiritual awakening? _____

_____
_____

⇒ TRIED TO CARRY THIS MESSAGE TO OTHERS

How have you tried to carry this message to otherse during your recovery? _____
_____
_____
_____

How do you intend to carry this message from here on? _____
_____
_____
_____

What are some things you have learned about yourself and others as you have carried the message to others?
_____
_____
_____
_____

What are some experiences you have had in "giving it away"?
_____
_____
_____
_____

How did you feel after giving it away in these experiences?

I felt _____

I felt _____

⇒ AND TO PRACTICE THESE PRINCIPLES IN ALL OUR AFFAIRS

The principles of honesty, spirituality, and responsibility for your own behavior, including promptly admitting wrongs, are all important. This is especially true as you continue to live a life-style of recovery so that you do not carry guilt and shame that could bring you back into a sexual addiction cycle. You deserve the best sobriety possible! In giving it away, you will find that your own recovery is enhanced.

How have you practiced these principles in the following areas of your life?

Spiritual Life

1. _____
2. _____
3. _____

Emotional Life

1. _____
2. _____
3. _____

Social Life

1. _____
2. _____
3. _____

Physical Health/Exercise

1. _____
2. _____
3. _____

Financially

1. _____
2. _____
3. _____

Parenting

1. _____
2. _____
3. _____

Work Relationships

1. _____
2. _____
3. _____

Family Members

1._____

2._____

3._____

Sexuality

1._____

2._____

3._____

Marriage

1._____

2._____

3._____

"Having had a spiritual awakening as the result of these Steps, we tried to carry this message to others, and to practice these principles in all our affairs." Do you feel you have fully experienced Step Twelve? Why or why not?

_____

_____

_____

_____

What is the most significant thing you learned about yourself completing Step Twelve?

_____

_____

_____

_____

On a scale from one to ten, rate yourself on Step Twelve.

1 2 3 4 5 6 7 8 9 10

Why?_____

_____

FEEDBACK FORM

The following space is provided for feedback from your group on your Step work. Use this feedback page for reflection or for continued work on your Step One. May your future journey of recovery begin with this first step.

Name of Group Member _____ Rating 1 2 3 4 5 6 7 8 9 10

Feedback _____

_____

_____

Name of Group Member _____ Rating 1 2 3 4 5 6 7 8 9 10

Feedback _____

_____

_____

Name of Group Member _____ Rating 1 2 3 4 5 6 7 8 9 10

Feedback _____

_____

_____

Name of Group Member _____ Rating 1 2 3 4 5 6 7 8 9 10

Feedback _____

_____

_____

Name of Group Member _____ Rating 1 2 3 4 5 6 7 8 9 10

Feedback _____

_____

_____

Name of Group Member _____ Rating 1 2 3 4 5 6 7 8 9 10

Feedback _____

_____

_____

APPENDIX

FEELINGS LIST

1. I feel (put word here) when (put a present situation when you feel this).
2. I first remember feeling (put the same feeling word here) when (explain earliest occurrence of this feeling)

RULES FOR COUPLES: 1- No examples about each other or the relationship. 2-Eye contact. 3-No feedback

Abandoned	Battered	Considerate	Distrusted	Goofy
Abused	Beaten	Consumed	Disturbed	Grateful
Aching	Beautiful	Content	Dominated	Greedy
Accepted	Belligerent	Cool	Domineering	Grief
Accused	Belittled	Courageous	Doomed	Grim
Accepting	Bereaved	Courteous	Doubtful	Grimy
Admired	Betrayed	Coy	Dreadful	Grouchy
Adored	Bewildered	Crabby	Eager	Grumpy
Adventurous	Blamed	Cranky	Ecstatic	Hard
Affectionate	Blaming	Crazy	Edgy	Harried
Agony	Bonded	Creative	Edified	Hassled
Alienated	Bored	Critical	Elated	Healthy
Aloof	Bothered	Criticized	Embarrassed	Helpful
Aggravated	Brave	Cross	Empowered	Helpless
Agreeable	Breathless	Crushed	Empty	Hesitant
Aggressive	Bristling	Cuddly	Enraged	High
Alive	Broken-up	Curious	Enraptured	Hollow
Alone	Bruised	Cut	Enthusiastic	Honest
Alluring	Bubbly	Damned	Enticed	Hopeful
Amazed	Burdened	Dangerous	Esteemed	Hopeless
Amused	Burned	Daring	Exasperated	Horrified
Angry	Callous	Dead	Excited	Hostile
Anguished	Calm	Deceived	Exhilarated	Humiliated
Annoyed	Capable	Deceptive	Exposed	Hurried
Anxious	Captivated	Defensive	Fake	Hurt
Apart	Carefree	Delicate	Fascinated	Hyper
Apathetic	Careful	Delighted	Feisty	Ignorant
Apologetic	Careless	Demeaned	Ferocious	Ignored
Appreciated	Caring	Demoralized	Foolish	Immature
Appreciative	Cautious	Dependent	Forced	Impatient
Apprehensive	Certain	Depressed	Forceful	Important
Appropriate	Chased	Deprived	Forgiven	Impotent
Approved	Cheated	Deserted	Forgotten	Impressed
Argumentative	Cheerful	Desirable	Free	Incompetent
Aroused	Childlike	Desired	Friendly	Incomplete
Astonished	Choked-up	Despair	Frightened	Independent
Assertive	Close	Despondent	Frustrated	Insecure
Attached	Cold	Destroyed	Full	Innocent
Attacked	Comfortable	Different	Funny	Insignificant
Attentive	Comforted	Dirty	Furious	Insincere
Attractive	Competent	Disenchanted	Gay	Isolated
Aware	Competitive	Disgusted	Generous	Inspired
Awestruck	Complacent	Disinterested	Gentle	Insulted
Badgered	Complete	Dispirited	Genuine	Interested
Baited	Confident	Distressed	Giddy	Intimate
Bashful	Confused	Distrustful	Giving	Intolerant

Copyright Douglas Weiss, Ph.D.   www.drdougweiss.com   719.278.3708

FEELINGS LIST

1. I feel (put word here) when (put a present situation when you feel this).
2. I first remember feeling (put the same feeling word here) when (explain earliest occurrence of this feeling)

RULES FOR COUPLES: 1- No examples about each other or the relationship. 2-Eye contact. 3-No feedback

Involved	Panicked	Respected	Stiff	Under control
Irate	Paralyzed	Restless	Stimulated	Understanding
Irrational	Paranoid	Revolved	Stifled	Understood
Irked	Patient	Riled	Strangled	Undesirable
Irresponsible	peaceful	Rotten	Strong	Unfriendly
Irritable	Pensive	Ruined	Stubborn	Ungrateful
Irritated	Perceptive	Sad	Stuck	Unified
Isolated	Perturbed	Safe	Stunned	Unhappy
Jealous	Phony	Satiated	Stupid	Unimpressed
Jittery	Pleasant	Satisfied	Subdued	Unsafe
Joyous	Pleased	Scared	Submissive	Unstable
Lively	Positive	Scolded	Successful	Upset
Lonely	Powerless	Scorned	Suffocated	Uptight
Loose	Present	Scrutinized	Sure	Used
Lost	Precious	Secure	Sweet	Useful
Loving	Pressured	Seduced	Sympathy	Useless
Low	Pretty	Seductive	Tainted	Unworthy
Lucky	Proud	Self-centered	Tearful	Validated
Lustful	Pulled apart	Self-conscious	Tender	Valuable
Mad	Put down	Selfish	Tense	Valued
Maudlin	Puzzled	Separated	Terrific	Victorious
Malicious	Quarrelsome	Sensuous	Terrified	Violated
Mean	Queer	Sexy	Thrilled	Violent
Miserable	Quiet	Shattered	Ticked	Voluptuous
Misunder-	Raped	Shocked	Tickled	Vulnerable
stood	Ravished	Shot down	Tight	Warm
Moody	Ravishing	Shy	Timid	Wary
Morose	Real	Sickened	Tired	Weak
Mournful	Refreshed	Silly	Tolerant	Whipped
Mystified	Regretful	Sincere	Tormented	Whole
Nasty	Rejected	Sinking	Torn	Wicked
Nervous	Rejuvenated	Smart	Tortured	Wild
Nice	Rejecting	Smothered	Touched	Willing
Numb	Relaxed	Smug	Trapped	Wiped out
Nurtured	Relieved	Sneaky	Tremendous	Wishful
Nuts	Remarkable	Snowed	Tricked	Withdrawn
Obsessed	Remem-	Soft	Trusted	Wonderful
Offended	bered	Solid	Trustful	Worried
Open	Removed	Solitary	Trusting	Worthy
Ornery	Repulsed	Sorry	Ugly	Wounded
Out of control	Repulsive	Spacey	Unacceptable	Young
Overcome	Resentful	Special	Unapproach-	Zapped
Overjoyed	Resistant	Spiteful	able	
Overpowered	Responsible	Spontaneous	Unaware	
Overwhelmed	Responsive	Squelched	Uncertain	
Pampered	Repressed	Starved	Uncomfortable	

Copyright Douglas Weiss, Ph.D.   www.drdougweiss.com   719.278.3708

THE TWELVE STEPS OF ALCOHOLICS ANONYMOUS

1. We admitted we were powerless over alcohol--that our lives had become unmanageable.

2. Came to believe that a Power greater than ourselves could restore us to sanity.

3. Made a decision to turn our will and our lives over to the care of God as we understood Him.

4. Made a searching and fearless moral inventory of ourselves.

5. Admitted to God, to ourselves, and to another human being the exact nature of our wrongs.

6. Were entirely ready to have God remove all these defects of character.

7. Humbly asked Him to remove our shortcomings.

8. Made a list of all people we had harmed, and became willing to make amends to them all.

9. Made direct amends to such people wherever possible, except when to do so would injure them or others.

10. Continued to take personal inventory, and when we were wrong, promptly admitted it.

11. Sought through prayer and meditation to improve our conscious contact with God as we understood Him, praying only for knowledge of His will for us and the power to carry that out.

12. Having had a spiritual awakening as the result of these steps, we tried to carry this message to others and to practice these principles in all our affairs.

The Twelve Steps reprinted for adaptation by permission of AA World Services, Inc. Copyright 1939.

THE TWELVE STEPS OF ALCOHOLICS ANONYMOUS ADAPTED FOR SEXUAL ADDICTS

1. We admitted we were powerless over our sexual addiction--that our lives had become unmanageable.

2. Came to believe that a Power greater than ourselves could restore us to sanity.

3. Made a decision to turn our will and our lives over to the care of God as we understood Him.

4. Made a searching and fearless moral inventory of ourselves.

5. Admitted to God, to ourselves, and to another human being the exact nature of our wrongs.

6. Were entirely ready to have God remove all these defects of character.

7. Humbly asked Him to remove our shortcomings.

8. Made a list of all people we had harmed, and became willing to make amends to them all.

9. Made direct amends to such people wherever possible, except when to do so would injure them or others.

10. Continued to take personal inventory, and when we were wrong, promptly admitted it.

11. Sought through prayer and meditation to improve our conscious contact with God as we understood Him, praying only for knowledge of His will for us and the power to carry that out.

12. Having had a spiritual awakening as the result of these steps, we tried to carry this message to others and to practice these principles in all our affairs.

COUNSELING

"Without the intensive, my marriage would have ended and I would not have known why. Now I am happier than ever and my marriage is bonded permanently."

Counseling Sessions

Couples are helped through critical phases of disclosure moving into the process of recovery, and rebuilding trust in relationships. We have helped many couples rebuild their relationship and grasp and implement the necessary skills for an intimate relationship.

Individual counseling offers a personal treatment plan for successful healing in your life. In just one session a counselor can help you understand how you became stuck and how to move toward freedom.

Partners of sex addicts need an advocate. Feelings of fear, hurt, anger, betrayal, and grief require a compassionate, effective response. We provide that expert guidance and direction. We have helped many partners heal through sessions that get them answers to their many questions including: "How can I trust him again?"

A counseling session today can begin your personal journey toward healing.

3 and 5 Day Intensives
in Colorado Springs, Colorado
are available for the following issues:

- Sexual Addiction Couple or Individual
- Marriage Intensives
- Partners of Sexual Addicts
- Intimacy Anorexia
- Victims of Sexual Abuse
- Adult Children of Sex Addicts
- Teenage Children of Sex Addicts

Attendees of Intensives will receive:

- Personal attention from counselors who specialize in your area of need
- An understanding of how the addiction /anorexia and its consequences came into being
- Three appointments daily
- Daily assignments to increase the productiveness of these daily sessions
- Individuals get effective counseling to recover from the effects of sexual addiction, abuse and anorexia
- Addiction, abuse, anorexia issues are thoroughly addressed for couples and individuals. This includes the effects on the partner or family members of the addict, and how to rebuild intimacy toward a stronger relationship.

www.drdougweiss.com 719.278.3708

NEW PRODUCTS

HEALING HER HEART AFTER RELAPSE

Relapse doesn't have to occur, but if it happens, knowing how to navigate it intelligently can make a huge difference in a marriage. Each relapse impacts the wife significantly. Every couple in recovery would do well to have these tools before a potential relapse.

DVD: $29.95

PAIN FOR LOVE

Pain For Love describes in detail one of the most insidious strategies of an intimacy anorexic with their spouse. This dynamic is experienced by many who are married to an intimacy anorexic. This paradigm can empower the spouse and help them stop participating in a pain for love dynamic in their marriage.

DVD: $29.95

SIN OF WITHHOLDING

This DVD is the first to address the Biblical foundation of the sin of withholding in believers' hearts. The practical application in marriage addressing Intimacy Anorexia is also interwoven in this revelational teaching on the Sin of Withholding. Once a believer is free of this sin, their walk with the Lord and their fruit towards others can increase expediently.

DVD: $49.95

NEW PRODUCTS

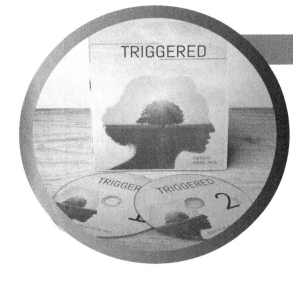

TRIGGERED

Triggers are normal for partners of sex addicts, but each woman's triggers are unique and must be navigated in different ways. This DVD can be a life-changing message which will validate your struggles to heal and help you face the challenges of being triggered after partner betrayal trauma.

DVD: $49.00

DISCLOSURE

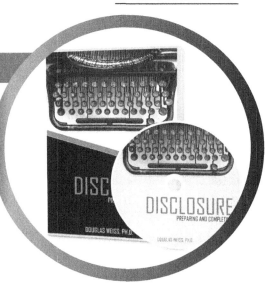

Disclosure is one of the most important topics in sexual addiction recovery. In this DVD, Dr. Weiss discusses the various types of disclosure. Each type of disclosure is for a specific purpose or person. This DVD can expedite the understanding of each of the significant processes of disclosure for the addict, the spouse and the marriage.

DVD: $39.95

BOUNDARIES

Boundaries are a healthy, normal, and necessary part of the recovery process for sex addicts, intimacy anorexics, and their spouses. In this DVD set, Dr. Doug Weiss provides an answer to the clarion call on boundaries by educating and guiding you through this process.

DVD: $49.95

MEN'S RECOVERY

This book gives more current information than many professional counselors have today. In addition to informing sex addicts and their partners about sex addiction, it gives hope for recovery. The information provided in this book would cost hundreds of dollars in counseling hours to receive. Many have attested to successful recovery from this information alone.

BOOK: $22.95
CD: $35.00

101 FREEDOM EXERCISES

This is the best single resource for the Christian who desires to know what they need to do to get and stay free from sexual addiction. This book contains 101 exercises that have been proven to work.

WORKBOOK: $39.95

STEPS TO FREEDOM

This is a Christian approach to the Twelve Steps. This book will guide you through the 12 Steps of recovery that have been helpful for many addicted people. This book is specifically written for the person desiring recovery from sexual addiction.

STEP BOOK: $14.95

HELPING HER HEAL

The *Helping Her Heal* DVD is for the man who has disclosed his sexual addiction to his partner or spouse. This DVD offers practical tools for hearing her pain, navigating her grief and losses, discovering her expectations of you and the boundaries she may need to heal.

DVD: $69.95

MARRIED AFTER ADDICTION

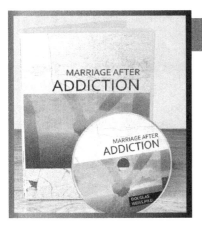

Addiction can have devastating effects on even good marriages. In this DVD you are intelligently guided through the journey you will experience if addiction is part of your marriage story. You will learn important information about the early and later stages of recovery for your marriage.

DVD: $29.95

SERIES FOR MEN

CLEAN

BOOK: $16.95
DVD: $29.95
JOURNAL: $16.95

Every Christian man is born into a sexual war. The enemy attacks the young, hoping to scar them permanently and leave them ruined. Your past is not enough to keep you from the enduringly clean life you want and deserve. This series can be used individually or in a small group setting.

LUST FREE LIVING

Every man can fight for and obtain a lust free lifestyle. Once you know how to stop lust, you will realize how weak lust really can be. God gace you the power to protect those you love from the ravages of lust for the rest of your life! It's time to take it back!

BOOK: $13.95
DVD: $23.95

MEN MAKE MEN

Dr. Weiss takes the listeners by the hand and step-by-step walks through the creative process God used to make every man into a man of God. This practical teaching on DVD combined with the Men Make Guidebook can revitalize the men in any home or local church.

DVD: $29.95
GUIDEBOOK: $11.95

WOMEN'S RECOVERY

Partners: Healing From His Addiction book is the latest in research of the affects on a woman who has lived with a sexual addict. The riveting statistics combined with personal stories of recovery make this a must read book for any woman in a relationship with a sex addict. This book gives you hope and a beginning plan for personal recovery.

BOOK: $14.95

PARTNER'S RECOVERY GUIDE

This is like therapy in a box for women who want to walk through the residual effects of being in a relationship with a sex addict.

WORKBOOK: $39.95

BEYOND LOVE

This is an interactive workbook that allows the partners of sex addicts to gain insight and strength through working the Twelve Steps.

STEP BOOK: $14.95

HE NEEDS TO CHANGE, DR. WEISS

He Needs To Change, Dr. Weiss DVD addresses the pain, trauma, and betrayal women experience because of their partner's sex addiction, betrayal, and/or intimacy anorexia. In this DVD, Dr. Weiss addresses the issue of change that he has explained to thousands of women in his office.

DVD: $29.95

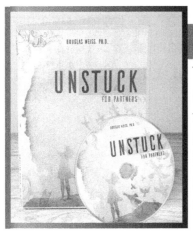

UNSTUCK FOR PARTNERS

The *Unstuck* DVD is for every woman who has experienced the pain of their partner's sex addiction or intimacy anorexia and feels stuck, confused, frustrated and unable to move on. You didn't sign up for this and honestly, you don't get it! This DVD helps you "get it" so you can process the painful reality you are in and start to live again.

DVD: $29.95

PARTNER BETRAYAL TRAUMA

Partner Betrayal Trauma is real. Your pain and experience of betrayal has impacted all of your being and all of your relationships.

The book, DVD set, Workbook and Step guide were designed to help guide you thoughtfully through your own personal healing from the effects of being betrayed by your spouse or significant other. The pain and trauma of being betrayed, especially sexual betrayal, by a spouse or significant other is multidimensional and multifaceted. Your pain and trauma are real and these resources will help you in your journey of recovery from Partner Betrayal Trauma.

BOOK: $22.95   DVD: $65.95   WORKBOOK: $39.95   STEPBOOK: $14.95

INTIMACY ANOREXIA

This hidden addiction is destroying so many marriages today. In your hands is the first antidote for someone with intimacy anorexia to turn the pages on this addiction process. Excerpts from intimacy anorexics and their spouses help this book become clinically helpful and personal in its impact to communicate hope and healing for the intimacy anorexic and the marriage.

BOOK: $22.95
DVD: $69.95

INTIMACY ANOREXIA: THE WORKBOOK

This is like therapy in a box. Inside is 100 exercises that have already been proven helpful in treating intimacy anorexia.

WORKBOOK: $39.95

INTIMACY ANOREXIA: THE STEPS

This is the only twelve step workbook just for intimacy anorexia. Each step gives you progress in your healing from intimacy anorexia.

STEP BOOK: $14.95

MARRIED & ALONE

This is for the spouse of an intimacy anorexic. You feel disconnected, untouched and often unloved. You are not crazy and Dr. Weiss will help you to start a journey of recovery from living with a spouse with intimacy anorexia.

BOOK: $14.95
DVD: $49.95

MARRIED & ALONE: HEALING EXERCISES FOR SPOUSES

This is the first workbook to offer practical suggestions and techniques to better navigate through recovery from your spouse's Intimacy Anorexia.

WORKBOOK: $39.95

MARRIED & ALONE: THE TWELVE STEP GUIDE

This Twelve Step guide will help the spouse of an intimacy anorexic work through the Twelve Steps that many others have found to be helpful in their recovery.

STEP BOOK: $14.95

MARRIAGE RESOURCES

LOVER SPOUSE

Lover Spouse helps you understand marriage from a Christ-centered perspective. Christian Marriages were designed to be different, passionate, fulfilling, and long-lasting.

BOOK: $13.95

UPGRADE YOUR SEX LIFE

Upgrade Your Sex Life actually teaches you own unique sexual expression that you and your partner are pre-wired to enjoy.

BOOK: $16.95

SERVANT MARRIAGE

Servant Marriage book is a Revelation on God's Masterpiece of marriage. In these pages, you will walk with God as He creates the man, the woman and his masterpiece called marriage.

BOOK: $13.95

MARRIAGE MONDAYS

This is an eight week marriage training that actually gives you the skills to have a healthy and more vibrant marriage.

BOOK: $16.95

INTIMACY

This 100 Day guide can transform couples from any level of intimacy to a lifestyle of satiation with their spouse.

BOOK: $11.95

MIRACLE OF MARRIAGE

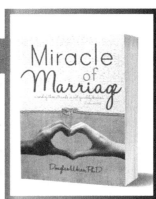

God made your marriage to be an amazing and unique miracle. Dr. Weiss walks you through the creation and maintenance of your marriage. You will be exposed to a practical insights that can help make your marriage into God's original design.

DVD: $12.95

OTHER RESOURCES

WORTHY: EXERCISES & STEP BOOK

The *Worthy* Workbook and DVD, is designed for a 12 week study. Here is a path that anyone can take to get and stay worthy. Follow this path, and you too will make the journey from worthless to worthy just as others have.

DVD: $29.95
BOOK: $29.95

EMOTIONAL FITNESS

Everyone has an unlimited number of emotions, but few have been trained to identify, choose, communicate, and master them. More than a guide for gaining emotional fitness and mastery, in these pages you will find a pathway to a much more fulfilling life.

BOOK: $16.95

LETTERS TO MY DAUGHTER

A gift for your daugher as she enters college. *Letters to my Daughter* includes my daily letters to my daughter during her first year of college.

BOOK: $14.95

BORN FOR WAR

Born for War teaches practical tools to defeat these sexual landmines and offers scriptural truths that empower young men to desire successfulness in the war thrust upon them.

DVD: $29.95

PRINCES TAKE LONGER THAN FROGS

This 2 hour DVD helps single women ages 15-30, to successfully navigate through the season of dating.

DVD: $29.95

SUCCESSFULLY SINGLE

This 2 Disc DVD Series is definitely nothing you have heard before. Dr. Weiss charts new territory as to the why for sexual purity.

DVD: $29.95

RECOVERY RESOURCES

Recovery for Everyone helps addicts fight and recover from any addiction they are facing. Learn truths and gain a biblical understanding to break the strongholds in your life.

You will also find an explanation as to how an addiction may have become a part of your life and details as to how you can walk the path to recovery. You will find a roadmap to help you begin and navigate an incredible journey toward freedom. Then you can become part of the solution and even help others get free as well.

BOOK: $22.95   DVD: $99.00   WORKBOOK: $39.95   STEPBOOK: $14.95

RESOURCES FOR FEMALE SEX ADDICTS

Secret Solutions is a practical recovery exercise workbook written specifically for female sex addicts. Many of these techniques have been used in private practice to help other female sex addicts.

WORKBOOK: $39.95

She has a Secret book is the most current book in the field of sex addiction for women and is packed with new statistics to further our understanding of female sexual addiction. This is a must-read for any woman struggling in this addiction as well as for professionals in this field.

BOOK: $14.95

Heart to Heart Counseling Center has recently acquired Cereset, the most technologically advanced neuromodulation software available. It has received 13 peer review publications, and 9 Institutional Review Boards (IRB) clinically approved trials including the US Military.

By rebalancing and recalibrating the brain, it has helped anxiety, PTSD, trauma, sleeplessness, addiction, low mood and energy, TBI, stress management and neuroplasticity in many of my clients. Most spouses at Heart to Heart Counseling Center have many of the PTSD symptoms from betrayal. More than 80% of those with addiction have unresolved traumas as part of their story.

The brain is your central command center. When your brain is out of balance, or stuck, you don't feel right and it's impossible to function at your highest level. Cereset is a proven technology that's non-invasive and highly effective. Cereset can help your brain free itself, enabling you to achieve higher levels of well-being and balance throughout your life.

Here's what clients had to say about Cereset Garden of the Gods after their sessions:

> "I'm waking up earlier and feeling more rested and alert. Anxiety is lessened. PTSD symptoms alleviated. Lessened food cravings and quantity of food reduced. Arthritis symptoms improved. I feel more relaxed, less angry and reactive."

The cost for five sessions (one per day) is $1,500.

For more information call us at 719-278-3708

A·A·S·A·T
American Association for Sex Addiction Therapy

SEX ADDICTION TRAINING SET

Both men and women are seeking to counsel more than ever for sexually addictive behaviors. You can be prepared! Forty-seven hours of topics related to sexual addiction treatment are covered in this training including:
- The Six Types of Sex Addicts
- Neurological Understanding
- Sex and Recovery
- Relapse Strategies

TRAINING SET: $1195

PARTNER'S RECOVERY TRAINING SET

With this AASAT training, you will gain proven clinical insight into treating the issues facing partners. You can be prepared! Thirty-nine hours of topics related to partners treatment are covered in this training, including:
- Partner Model
- Partner Grief
- Anger
- Boundaries

TRAINING SET: $995

INTIMACY ANOREXIA TRAINING SET

This growing issue of Intimacy Anorexia will need your competent help in your community. Now, you can be prepared to identify it and treat it. In this training you'll cover topics like:
- Identifying Intimacy Anorexia
- Causes of Intimacy Anorexia
- Treatment Plan
- Relapse Strategies

TRAINING SET: $995

FOR MORE INFORMATION VISIT WWW.AASAT.ORG OR CALL 719.330.2425

Made in the USA
Middletown, DE
11 June 2022

66893992R00073